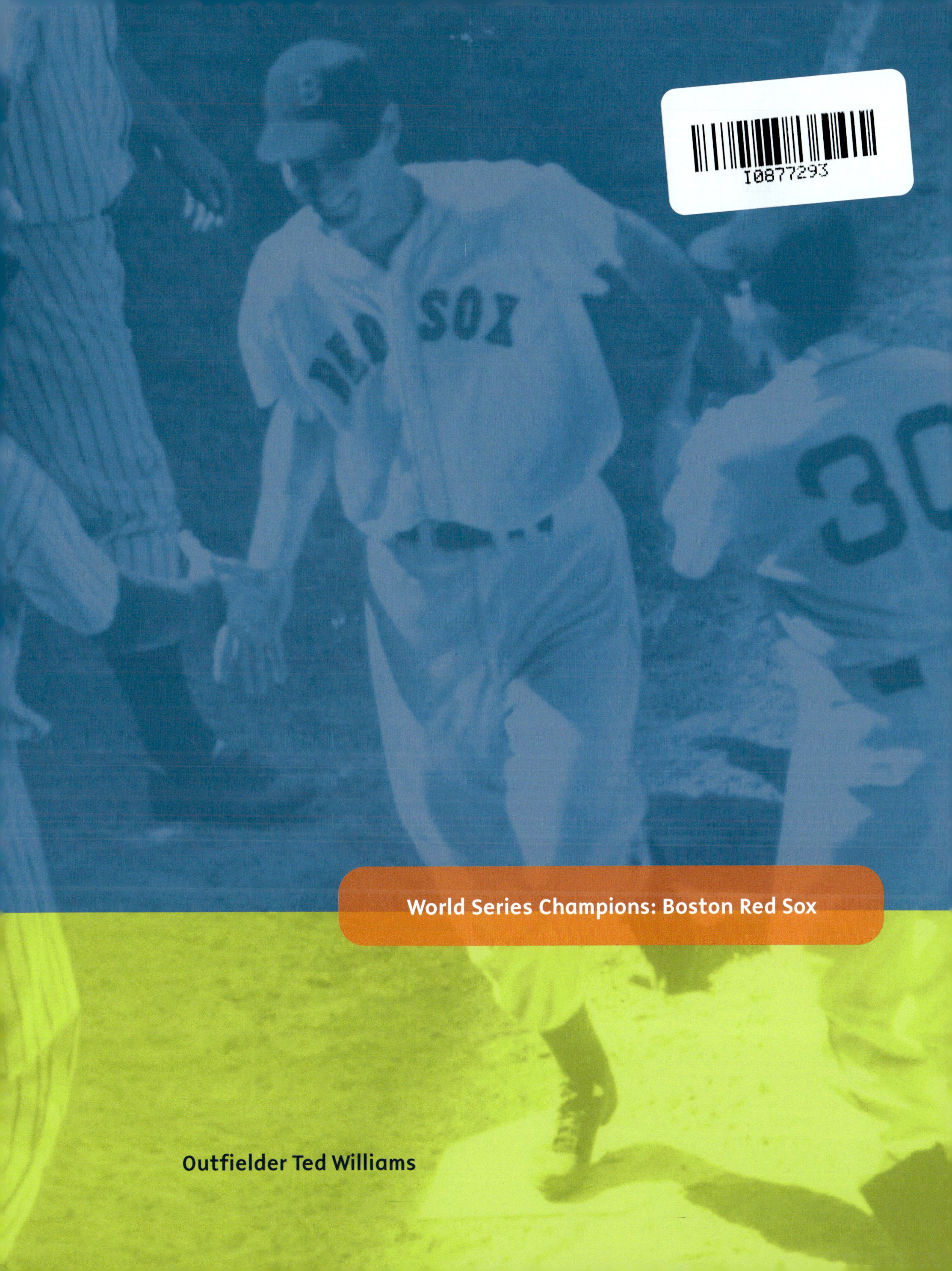

World Series Champions: Boston Red Sox

Outfielder Ted Williams

Outfielder Jim Rice

WORLD SERIES CHAMPIONS

BOSTON RED SOX

MICHAEL E. GOODMAN

CREATIVE SPORTS

CREATIVE EDUCATION / CREATIVE PAPERBACKS

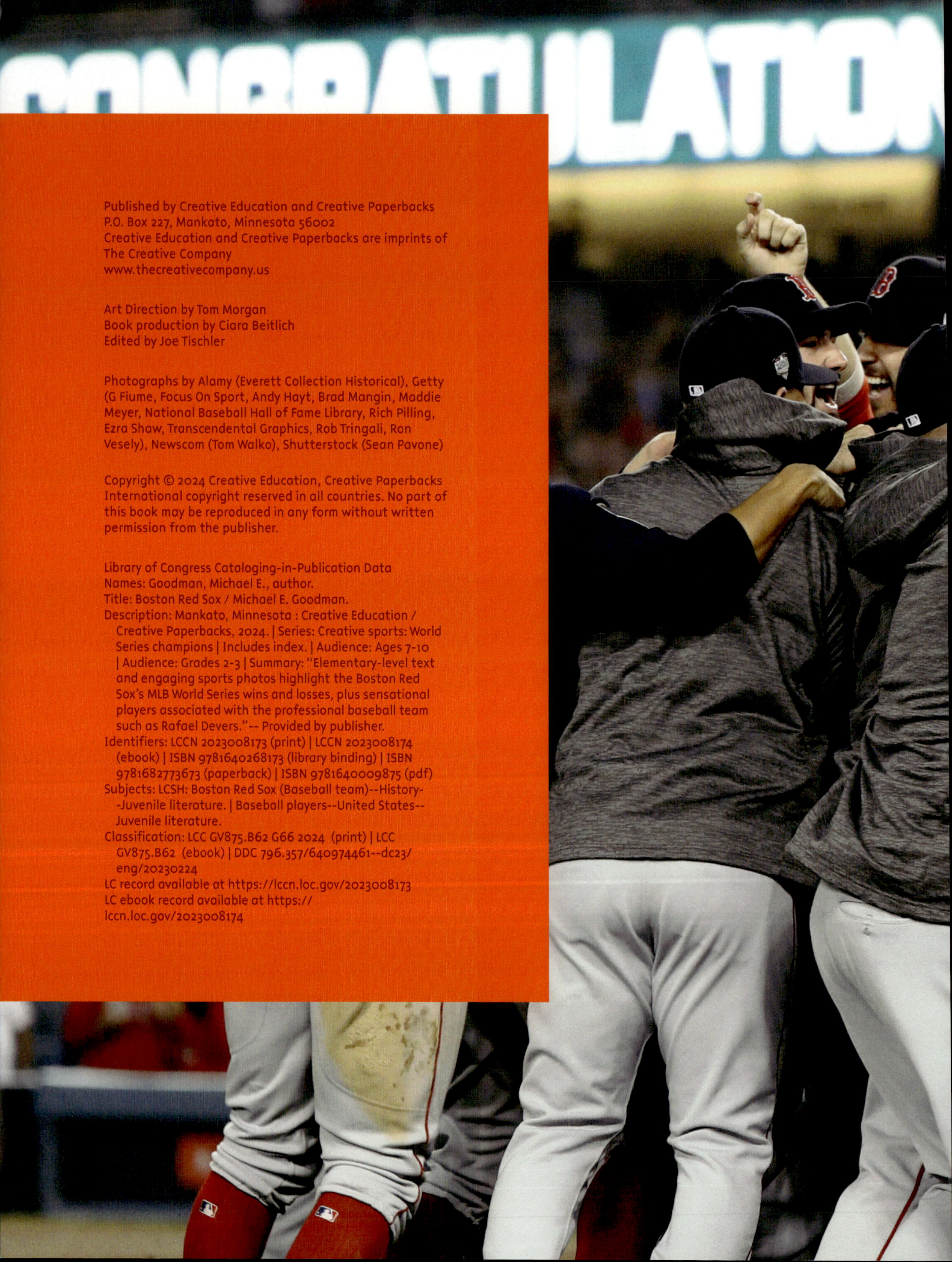

Published by Creative Education and Creative Paperbacks
P.O. Box 227, Mankato, Minnesota 56002
Creative Education and Creative Paperbacks are imprints of The Creative Company
www.thecreativecompany.us

Art Direction by Tom Morgan
Book production by Ciara Beitlich
Edited by Joe Tischler

Photographs by Alamy (Everett Collection Historical), Getty (G Fiume, Focus On Sport, Andy Hayt, Brad Mangin, Maddie Meyer, National Baseball Hall of Fame Library, Rich Pilling, Ezra Shaw, Transcendental Graphics, Rob Tringali, Ron Vesely), Newscom (Tom Walko), Shutterstock (Sean Pavone)

Library of Congress Cataloging-in-Publication Data
Names: Goodman, Michael E., author.
Title: Boston Red Sox / Michael E. Goodman.
Description: Mankato, Minnesota : Creative Education / Creative Paperbacks, 2024. | Series: Creative sports: World Series champions | Includes index. | Audience: Ages 7-10 | Audience: Grades 2-3 | Summary: "Elementary-level text and engaging sports photos highlight the Boston Red Sox's MLB World Series wins and losses, plus sensational players associated with the professional baseball team such as Rafael Devers."-- Provided by publisher.
Identifiers: LCCN 2023008173 (print) | LCCN 2023008174 (ebook) | ISBN 9781640268173 (library binding) | ISBN 9781682773673 (paperback) | ISBN 9781640009875 (pdf)
Subjects: LCSH: Boston Red Sox (Baseball team)--History--Juvenile literature. | Baseball players--United States--Juvenile literature.
Classification: LCC GV875.B62 G66 2024 (print) | LCC GV875.B62 (ebook) | DDC 796.357/640974461--dc23/eng/20230224
LC record available at https://lccn.loc.gov/2023008173
LC ebook record available at https://lccn.loc.gov/2023008174

2018 World Series Champions

Outfielder Tris Speaker

CONTENTS

Home of the Red Sox

Boston, Massachusetts, is one of the oldest cities in the United States. It was founded in 1630. Boston's baseball team also has a long history. The Red Sox play at a **stadium** called Fenway Park. They have been playing games there for more than 110 years.

The Boston Red Sox are a Major League Baseball (MLB) team. They play in the American League (AL) East Division. Their biggest **rivals** are the New York Yankees. All MLB teams try to win the World Series to become champions. The Red Sox have won nine World Series **titles**.

Outfielder/Pitcher Babe Ruth

Naming the Red Sox

The AL was formed in 1901. The Boston Americans were one of its first teams. The players wore bright red socks. In 1908, the team's name changed to Red Sox. Today's home uniforms are white with red letters. Hats are navy blue with a red *B* on the front.

Pitcher Cy Young

Red Sox History

The Boston Americans began winning right away. In 1903, they finished first in the AL. They competed against the Pittsburgh Pirates in the first World Series. Boston won 5 games to 3. Star pitcher Cy Young was a hero in the series.

Boston won four more titles over the next 15 years. Two stars were hard-hitting outfielders Tris Speaker and Babe Ruth. Ruth was also the team's leading pitcher. Then Ruth's contract was sold to the Yankees. The Red Sox went into a long **slump**. They did not win another title for 86 years!

During the slump, the Red Sox reached the World Series four times. They lost each series 4 games to 3. In 1986, they were one out from winning. Then, an error cost them the game. Boston fans worried that their team would never be champs again.

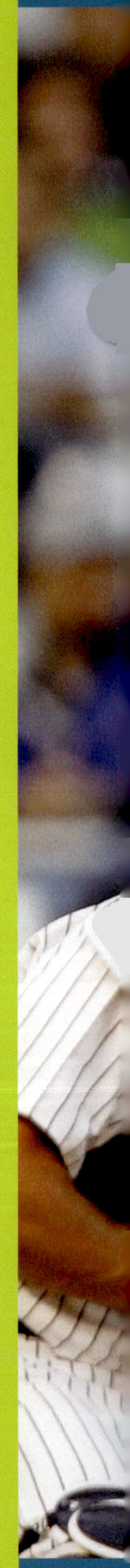

Designated hitter David Ortiz

Pitcher Pedro Martínez

In the 2000s, the Red Sox won big. They earned titles in 2004, 2007, 2013, and 2018. Two stars were solid designated hitter David Ortiz and tricky pitcher Pedro Martínez. Both were later elected to the Baseball **Hall of Fame**.

Other Red Sox Stars

Red Sox fans have cheered for many great hitters. Outfielder Ted Williams is the last batter to hit over .400 in a season. Outfielder Carl Yastrzemski (*yaz-STREM-skee*) hit for the **Triple Crown** in 1967. Outfielder Jim Rice batted over .300 seven times. Third baseman Wade Boggs led the AL in batting average five times.

Third baseman Wade Boggs

Outfielder Alex Verdugo

New hitting stars Rafael Devers and Alex Verdugo. Fans hope they can help bring more World Series banners to Fenway Park soon.

About the Red Sox

Started playing: 1901

League/division: American League, East Division

Team colors: navy blue and red

Home stadium: Fenway Park

WORLD SERIES CHAMPIONSHIPS:

1903, 5 games to 3 over Pittsburgh Pirates

1912, 4 games to 3 over New York Giants

1915, 4 games to 1 over Philadelphia Phillies

1916, 4 games to 1 over Brooklyn Robins

1918, 4 games to 2 over Chicago Cubs

2004, 4 games to 0 over St. Louis Cardinals

2007, 4 games to 0 over Colorado Rockies

2013, 4 games to 2 over St. Louis Cardinals

2018, 4 games to 1 over Los Angeles Dodgers

Boston Red Sox website: www.mlb.com/redsox

Glossary

Hall of Fame—a museum in which the best players of all time are honored

rival—a team that plays extra hard against another team

slump—a period of time in which a team plays poorly and loses often

stadium—a building with tiers of seats for spectators

title—another word for championship

Triple Crown—the honor of leading the league in batting average, home runs, and runs batted in (RBI) in the same season

Third baseman Rafael Devers

Index